HEAVENLY ANGEL

LAY LAY

EXPLAINS WHAT

'MANY ARE CALLED,

BUT FEW ARE CHOSEN'

REALLY MEANS

PUBLISHING COMPANY

ISBN: 978-0-6151-7487-7

www.crossover-ministries-publishing.com

TABLE OF CONTENTS

MANY ARE CALLED, BUT FEW ARE CHOSEN

MOSES

BIBLIOGRAPHY

ABOUT THE AUTHOR

I was dedicated to Jesus Christ of Nazareth as an infant and accepted Him as my Lord and Savior around seven years old when a visiting youth group led me in prayer at the alter. During my Salvation Prayer I asked Jesus to use me in a special ministry. Something that very few other Christians would want to do. I saw all the people just sitting in the pews, the ushers, and the Sunday School teachers and realized any Christian could do that. I wanted something different. One day in church service there was a visiting minister at a church I was visiting as well. The Minister said, "Jesus is going to make you a 'Healer of a Heart'". Then he asked me if I knew what that meant. I said, "No." the minister said, "I don't either, but whatever it is, Jesus is going to use you in a powerful way.

Helping Rachael, Jesus showed me what a 'Healer of the Heart' is. During the course of me helping Rachael to the 'Promised Land', a real Heavenly Angel named Lay Lay and I were allowed one hour one day to talk about Spiritual and Family situations from the King James Version of the Word of God. These books are designed to answer a lot of Spiritual Questions not even your minister can answer or your Church Denomination. I know theology Doctors who can't tell you how people other than Noah and his family made it past the 'Great Flood', yet their names are listed in the King James Version of the Word of God right after the 'World Wide Flood'. These books explain that and much more. I have written these books to tell the whole truth about the Word of God no matter how difficult it may be for me or others. Yes, there are things I write in these books that I don't even like, but in all fairness and total honestly, I must say the WHOLE TRUTH. The title of this book is 100% real. HEAVENLY ANGEL LAY LAY explained to me why gays, lesbians, bi-sexuals, and transsexuals DO NOT go to Heaven. I know this may make some people mad, but I won't 'Candy Coat' the Word of the Living God or what any Heavenly Angel said to me.

INTRODUCTION

The first section of this book talks about the scripture, 'Many are called, but few are chosen' really means. The second section of this book tells about Moses. All scriptures are taken from the King James Version of the Word of God. This book contains an excerpt from my book. MATTHEW'S WORD 'TWO':REAL WORD OF GOD BIBLE.

BOOKS WRITTEN BY WALTER BURCHETT, BA:

MATTHEW'S WORD 'TWO':REAL WORD OF GOD BIBLE   ISBN: 1-4116-6995-9

HEAVENLY ANGEL LAY LAY EXPLAINS WHY ADAM WAS NEVER CURSED
                                              ISBN: 978-1-84728-176-0

HEAVENLY ANGEL LAY LAY EXPLAINS WHY ABORTED BABIES DO NOT GO TO HEAVEN
                                              ISBN: 978-0-6151-7470-9

HEAVENLY ANGEL LAY LAY EXPLAINS THE BIBLICAL GROUNDS FOR MARRIAGE,
          SEPARATION, AND DIVORCE   ISBN: 978-0-6151-7481-5

HEAVENLY ANGEL LAY LAY EXPLAINS WHY PROFESSIONAL COUNSELORS HAVE 'HARDENED
          HEARTS'   ISBN: 978-0-6151-7482-2

HEAVENLY ANGEL LAY LAY EXPLAINS THE DIFFERENCE BETWEEN A 'COLD CHRISTIAN' AND
          A 'BACKSLIDER'   ISBN: 978-0-6151-7483-9

HEAVENLY ANGEL LAY LAY EXPLAINS WHICH BIBLE TO READ, WHICH BIBLE NOT TO READ,
          AND WHY   ISBN: 978-0-6151-7484-6

HEAVENLY ANGEL LAY LAY EXPLAINS WHY GAYS, LESBIANS, BI-SEXUALS, AND
          TRANSSEXUALS DO NOT GO TO HEAVEN   ISBN: 978-0-6151-7485-3

HEAVENLY ANGEL LAY LAY EXPLAINS WHY CHILDREN AND SPORTS ARE DEFINITELY A
          RELIGION IN TODAY'S SOCIETY   ISBN: 978-0-6151-7486-0

HEAVENLY ANGEL LAY LAY EXPLAINS WHAT 'MANY ARE CALLED, BUT FEW ARE CHOSEN
          REALLY MEANS   ISBN: 978-0-6151-7487-7

HEAVENLY ANGEL LAY LAY AND GUARDIAN ANGEL SHADOW GUESS THE REAL AGE OF THE
          EARTH   ISBN: 978-0-6151-7488-4

AN ABUSED MAN'S BATTLES, TRYING TO PROTECT HIS BOYS   ISBN: 978-0-6151-5191-5

HEAVENLY ANGEL

LAY LAY

EXPLAINS WHAT

'MANY ARE CALLED, BUT FEW ARE CHOSEN' REALLY MEANS

'MANY ARE CALLED, BUT FEW ARE CHOSEN'

I asked, "What about the verse, 'Many are called but few are chosen.' A lot of Christians think that means Jesus calls a lot of Christians to be Ordained Ministers and yet He only chooses a few. Others think it means those from within a certain church belief will only make it into Heaven." Lay Lay said, "No, They think that because they aren't reading the whole scripture about that particular verse like I pointed out before. Different churches use that part of the scripture to filter out Christians who that particular denomination wants and doesn't want behind their own pulpits. Who are denominations to say who the Father in Heaven does and does not call to spread the Gospel of Jesus? That's what got the girls confused to begin with, all the different 'church doctrines' that churches kept pushing on them instead of just witnessing to the individual about how wonderful it is to worship and serve Jesus. It's not a wonder there are so many humans who don't want to get involved in any church, the churches don't stop and think that those humans have never studied like the 'high up in the denomination' has so the doctrines blow the newcomer right out of the water. All the members in the churches do is take the word of the 'high up in the denomination' and take their word for what the King James Version of the Word of God says, there are a lot of denominations who have changed their minds about what the book of Revelation means even from 50 years ago. If they knew the truth the first time, then why did they change their minds and change their doctrine? You have gone to ministers in the smaller churches and shown them scriptures, explained the scriptures to them and they put you on hold, but if their denomination send that same scripture down through the chain, that same minister would take their word for the same meaning you said and not question the meaning. What it amounts to is a lot of ministers today don't take the time to research the scriptures or ask the Holy Spirit to teach them, they take the word of their denomination without question. What that scripture really means is the Israelites were the 'chosen people' called at first, and since the Nation of Israel refused to come to Jesus, only a few of them are actually 'chosen' to be at the Marriage Supper of the Lamb. Now everyone is called or invited to the Marriage Supper of the Lamb, as I said before. Jesus promised that everyone will be told about Him. That's why the Holy Spirit placed it upon your heart to 'instant message' 'MrsBadluck' to begin with. Jesus had to keep His promise to Rachael to inform her about Him so Rachael could choose who she wanted to serve for all eternity. The parable says the servants went out and told 'everyone', all God's creation. Now it's a universal call to everyone, to come to the 'Marriage Supper of the Lamb'. The parable talks about the King seeing a man without a 'Robe of Righteousness' on and asking the man, 'Friend, how camest thou in hither not having a wedding garment? And he was speechless. In other words, that man didn't accepted Jesus as his Lord and Savior and there was no excuse good enough to tell the Father in Heaven why he didn't, in his defense on Judgment Day. Although he was invited, he chose to believe he could go to the Marriage Supper through the Laws of the Old Testament, without a 'Robe of Righteousness' that a Christian receives through Jesus. Meaning on Judgment Day those who try to get into Heaven without accepting Jesus as their Lord and Savior will be cast into Hell because they won't have on the 'Robe of Righteousness'. Like Catholics worshipping the Statue of Mary. They won't make it into the Kingdom of Heaven because they are worshipping the Idol of Mary the mother of Jesus, Mary is like Father Abraham. Mary doesn't have any power to go through her Earthly son even though He is the Son of the Living God. Mary was the human mother of Jesus, but that's all she was. If Christians would stop and think about it, Mary didn't even raise Jesus after Jesus was of age for the man to take over with the boys back then. It was the custom that the father raise the son, Joseph is actually the raiser and human teacher of Jesus. Joseph is also how Jesus Himself was known as the Carpenter's Son and the Carpenter, Joseph was the Carpenter and by trade so was Jesus, not Mary. A human doesn't learn a trade overnight, after a few years of human life, Jesus spent much more time with Joseph than with Mary because the father is the teacher of the family. If the teachers in the temple were amazed by Jesus questions and answers, how could Mary answer them? Basically Mary only knew what Mary's father and Joseph taught her, the basics. After a while Joseph and Mary were both learning from Jesus

Himself. Jesus didn't start His ministry until He was in His 30's, and Jesus wasn't always playing with the children, His mind was always thinking about the scriptures of the Old Testament. You can tell that by what happened to Jesus when He was 12 years old in the temple doing His Father's Business.

Luke 2:40-52 (KJV)
40) And the child grew, and waxed strong in spirit, filled with wisdom: and the grace of God was upon him.
41) Now his parents went to Jerusalem every year at the feast of the passover.
42) And when **he was TWELVE YEARS OLD**, they went up to Jerusalem after the custom of the feast.
43) And when they had fulfilled the days, as they returned, the child Jesus tarried behind in Jerusalem; and Joseph and his mother knew not of it.
44) But they, supposing him to have been in the company, went a day's journey; and they sought him among their kinsfolk and acquaintance.
45) And when they found him not, they turned back again to Jerusalem, seeking him.
46) And it came to pass, that after three days they found him in the temple, sitting in the midst of the doctors, both hearing them, and asking them questions.
47) And **all** that heard him **were astonished** at **his understanding and answers**.
48) And when they saw him, they were amazed: and his mother said unto him, Son, why hast thou thus dealt with us? behold, thy father and I have sought thee sorrowing.
49) And he said unto them, How is it that ye sought me? wist ye not that **I must be about MY FATHER'S BUSINESS?**
50) And they understood not the saying which he spake unto them.
51) And he went down with them, and came to Nazareth, and was subject unto them: but his mother kept all these sayings in her heart.
52) And Jesus increased in wisdom and stature, and in favour with God and man.

Mark 6:1-3 (KJV)
1) And he went out from thence, and came into his own country; and his disciples follow him.
2) And when the sabbath day was come, he began to teach in the synagogue: and many hearing him were astonished, saying, From whence hath this man these things? and what wisdom is this which is given unto him, that even such mighty works are wrought by his hands?
3) **Is not this the CARPENTER**, the son of Mary, the brother of James, and Joses, and of Juda, and Simon? and are not his sisters here with us? And they were offended at him.

      Mary, the mother of Jesus, is now the fiancée of Jesus just like all other Christians, nothing more and nothing less, just like Father Abraham. Neither Father Abraham or Mary can intercede for any human, they don't have that power. Interceding for humans to the Father in Heaven is Jesus's job. If either Father Abraham or Mary could intercede for a human now, then Jesus Himself wouldn't have had to be Crucified and Resurrected to become human's intercessor to begin with. 'Binding the man hand and feet' simply means there will be no way for him to get out of Hell once he is there. In human terms, there is 'no appeal'. The first decision of the Father in Heaven, the Judge, is Final. People like that will be in the Lake of Fire, Hell for all eternity. There will be no sin in Heaven. 'But few are chosen' means, only those Israelites who came forward on an individual basis and truly accepted Jesus as their Lord and Savior are 'chosen'. God gave the Israelites several chances to be His Chosen People all the way through the Old Testament. He kept warning them, as a nation they kept coming back and leaving again. Then during the silent years, the Nation of Israel fell again. When Jesus came to Earth, as a nation they didn't come forward. Even after Jesus told them, 'I am here, come to me now', they still didn't come. That's when Jesus said this particular parable changing the Chosen People from the Nation of Israel to individuals from the Nation of Israel and any Gentiles who chose to come forward as well, just as the Father in Heaven warned in the Old Testament was going to happen if they didn't come back as a nation, and continue doing as He said then needed to do for Him to be their God. Just like the Pharisees and Sadducees didn't believe and didn't come forward. That's how Jesus was sentenced to be crucified to begin with, the Nation of Israel didn't believe Jesus was the Messiah, the Son of the Living God, they called him a 'false prophet' and a 'blasphemer' at times.

Jeremiah 3:6-10 (KJV)
6) The Lord said also unto me in the days of Josiah the king, Hast thou seen *that* which <u>backsliding Israel</u> hath done? She is gone up upon every high mountain and under every green tree, and there hath played the harlot.
7) And I said after she had done all these *things*, <u>Turn thou unto me. But she returned not.</u> And her treacherous sister Judah saw *it*.
8) And I saw, when for all the causes whereby backsliding **ISRAEL COMMITTED ADULTERY I had put her away, and given her a BILL OF DIVORCE** (No longer God's chosen nation); yet her treacherous sister Judah feared not, but went and played the harlot also. (God is talking about Spiritual Adultery, worshipping Idols and false Gods)
        Jeremiah 3:14 (KJV) *Turn, O backsliding children, saith the Lord;* ***for I AM MARRIED UNTO YOU:*** *and I will take you one of a city, and two of a family, and I will bring you to Zion:*
9) And it came to pass through the lightness of her whoredom, that she defiled the land, and **COMMITTED ADULTERY WITH STONES AND (IDOLS) WITH STOCKS (ANIMALS).   (WORSHIPPING IDOLS AND SATAN INSTEAD OF GOD)**
10) And yet for all this her treacherous sister <u>Judah hath not turned unto me with her whole heart, but feignedly</u> (falsely), saith the Lord.
        That's why Tony had to say the Sinner's Prayer the second time. He really didn't accept Jesus as his Lord and Savior the first time. He said the words for the girls, but not for himself and not from his heart."

Jeremiah 3:20) ***Surely as a WIFE treacherously*** <u>***departeth from her husband***</u>***, so have ye dealt treacherously with me, O house of Israel, saith the Lord.***

Jeremiah 21:27-31 (KJV)
27) Behold, the days come saith the Lord, that I will sow the house of

Israel and the house of Judah with the seed of man, and with the seed of beast.

28) And it shall come to pass, *that* like as I have watched over them, to pluck up, and to break down, and to throw down, and to destroy, and to afflict; so will I watch over them, to build, and to plant, saith the Lord.

29) In those days they shall say no more, The fathers have eaten a sour grape, and the children's teeth are set on edge.

30) **But every one shall die FOR HIS OWN INIQUITY:** every man that eateth the sour grape, his teeth shall be set on edge. (Warning that they will no longer be God's chosen people as a Nation, but as individuals they will be judged)

31) Behold, the days come, saith the Lord, that I will make a new covenant with the house of Israel, and with the house of Judah:

Matthew 26:27-28 (KJV)

27) And he took the cup, and gave thinks, and gave it to them saying, *Drink ye all of it;*

28) For this is my blood of the new testament, which is shed for many for the remission of sins. (All who accept Jesus as their Lord and Savior is in the New Covenant, the 'Spiritual Blood Line')

Jeremiah 21:32-37 (KJV)

32) Not according to the covenant that I made with their fathers in the day *that* I took them by the hand to bring them out of the land of Egypt; **which my covenant they brake,** although I was an husband unto them, saith the Lord:

33) But this *shall be* **the covenant** that I will make with the house of Israel; **after those days,** saith the Lord, **I will put my law in their hearts; and will be their God, and they shall be my people.** (This is only if the house of Israel truly comes to Jesus for their salvation as a nation, not like Tony did the first time. Notice the scripture says, 'SHALL BE', He is giving them a choice.)

34) And they shall teach no more every man his neighbour, and every man his brother, saying, Know the Lord: for they shall all know me, from the least of them unto the greatest of them, saith the Lord: for I will forgive

their iniquity, and I will remember their sin no more.

35) Thus saith the Lord, which giveth the sun for a light by day, *and* the ordinances of the moon and of the stars for a light by night, which divideth the sea when the waves thereof roar: The Lord of hosts is his name:

36) **If those ordinances depart from before me, saith the Lord, THEN THE SEED OF ISRAEL ALSO SHALL CEASE FROM BEING A NATION BEFORE ME FOREVER.** (The consequences if the Nation of Israel does not come to Jesus for their salvation.)

37) Thus saith the Lord; If heaven above can be measured, and the foundations of the earth searched out beneath, **I will also CAST OFF ALL THE SEED OF ISRAEL FOR ALL THAT THEY HAVE DONE, saith the Lord.**

Ezekiel 18:25-30 (KJV)

25) Yet ye say, The way of the Lord is not Equal. Hear now, O house of Israel: Is not my way equal? Are not your ways unequal?

26) When a righteous *man* turneth away from his righteousness, and committeth iniquity, and dieth in them; for his iniquity that he hath done shall he die.

27) Again, when the wicked *man* turneth away from his wickedness that he hath committed, and doeth that which is lawful and right, he shall save his soul alive.

28) Because he considereth, and turneth away from all his transgressions that he hath committed, he shall surely live, he shall not die.

29) Yet saith the house of Israel, The way of the Lord is not equal. O house of Israel, are not my ways equal? Are not your ways unequal?

30) **THEREFORE I WILL JUDGE YOU, O HOUSE OF ISRAEL,** *EVERYONE ACCORDING TO HIS WAYS,* saith the Lord God. **REPENT, AND TURN** *YOURSELVES* **FROM ALL YOUR TRANSGRESSIONS, SO INIQUITY SHALL NOT BE YOUR RUIN.**

Ezekiel 18:31, 32) (KJV)

31) Cast away from you all your transgressions, whereby ye had transgressed: and make you a new heart and a new spirit: for why will ye die, O house of Israel?

32) For I have no pleasure in the death of him that dieth, saith the Lord God: wherefore turn *yourselves*, and live ye.

Again in Ezekiel 33:17-20 (KJV)
17) Yet the children of thy people say, The way of the Lord is not equal: but as for them, their way is not equal.
18) When the righteous turneth from his righteousness, and committeth iniquity, he shall even die thereby,
19) But if the wicked turn from his wickedness; and do that which is lawful and right, he shall live thereby.
20) Yet ye say, The way of the Lord is not equal. **O Israel, I will judge you every one after his ways.**

Matthew 15:21-29 (KJV), Mk 7:24-30 (KJV),
Matthew 15:21 Then Jesus went thence, and departed into the coasts of Tyre and Sidon.
Mark 7:24 And from thence he arose, and went into the borders of Tyre and Sidon, and entered into an house, and would have no man know *it*: but he could not be hid.

Matthew 15:22 (First part) And, behold, a woman of Canaan came out of the same coasts, and cried unto him, saying have mercy on me,
Mark.7:26 The woman was a Greek, a Syrophenician by nation; and she besought him that he would cast forth the devil out of her daughter.

Matthew 15:22 (Second Part) O Lord *thou* Son of David; my daughter is grievously vexed with a devil.
Mark. 7:25 For a *certain* woman, whose young daughter had an unclean spirit, heard him, and came and fell at his feet:

Matthew 15:23 But he answered her not a word. And his disciples came and besought him, saying, Send her away; for she crieth after us.
Matthew 15:24 But he answered and said, I am not sent but unto the lost sheep of the house of Israel.
Matthew 15:25 Then came she and worshipped him, saying, Lord, help me.

Matthew 15:26 But he answered and said, It is not meet to take the children's bread, and to cast it to the dogs.'

Mark. 7:27 But Jesus said unto her, Let the children first be filled: for it is not meet to take the children's bread, and to cast *it* unto the dogs.

Matthew. 15:27 And she said, Truth, Lord: yet the dogs eat of the crumbs which fall from their master's table. (This is when Jesus started ministering to all the people, not just to the Israelites.)

Mark. 7:28 And she answered and said unto him, Yes, Lord: yet the dogs under the table eat of the children's crumbs. (This is when Jesus started ministering to all the people, not just to the Israelites.)

Matthew 15:28 Then Jesus answered and said unto her, 'O woman, great is thy faith: *be it unto thee even as thou wilt.'* and her daughter was made whole from that very hour.

Mark. 7:29 and he said unto her, For this saying go thy way; the devil is gone out of thy daughter.

Mark. 7:30 And when she was come to her house, she found the devil gone out, and her daughter laid upon the bed."

       Lay Lay continued, "It was just after that when Jesus changed the 'Physical Bloodline' to a 'Spiritual Bloodline'.

Matthew 22:1-14 (KJV)

1) And Jesus answered and spake unto them again by parables, and said,

2) The kingdom of heaven is like unto a certain king, which made a marriage for his son.

3) And sent forth his servants to call them that were bidden to the wedding: and they would not come. (The Nation of Israel as a nation.)

4) Again, he sent forth other servants, saying. Tell them which are bidden, Behold, I have prepared my dinner: my oxen and *my* fatling *are* killed, and all things *are* ready: come unto the marriage.

5) But they made light of *it* (The Nation of Israel), and went their ways, one to his farm, another to his merchandise:

6) And the remnant took his servants (Prophets), and entreated *them* spitefully, and slew *them*.

7) But when the king heard *thereof,* he was wroth: and he sent forth his

armies, and destroyed those murderers, and burned up their city.

8) Then saith he to his servants, The wedding is ready, but they which were bidden were not worthy. (Nation of Israel is not worthy as a Nation.)

9) Go ye therefore into the highways, and as many as ye shall find, bid to the marriage. (Opening salvation up for all who wish to go to Heaven through Jesus. Jews and Gentiles alike.)

10) So those servants went out into the highways, and gathered together all as many as they found, both bad and good: and the wedding was furnished with guests.

11) And when the king came in to see the guests, he saw there a man which had not on a wedding garment: (A sinner, not a Christian. Someone who had not accepted Jesus as their Lord and Savior yet)

12) And he saith unto him, Friend, how camest thou in hither not having a wedding garment? And he was speechless.

13) Then said the king to the servants, Bind him hand and foot, and take him away, and cast *him* into outer darkness; there shall be weeping and gnashing of teeth.

14) For many are called, but few are chosen. (This stipulates that many, an infinite number, of the Children of Israel are called, even today they are being called, but few are chosen because few accept Jesus as their Lord and Savior which is necessary to enter into the Kingdom of Heaven. This whole parable is talking about the Children of Israel as a nation that doesn't make it and those individual Israelites who do accept Jesus as their Lord and Savior do make it from each tribe of Israel.)

Acts 13:44-52 (KJV)

44) And the next Sabbath day came almost the whole city together to hear the word of God.

45) But when the Jews saw the multitudes, they were filled with envy, and spake against those things which were spoken by Paul, contradicting and blaspheming. (The Jews were jealous because Paul and Barnabas drew a huge crowd, more people then came to see them.)

46) Then Paul and Barnabas waxed bold, and said, It was necessary that the word of God should first have been spoken to you: but seeing ye put it from you, and judge yourselves unworthy of everlasting life, **lo, we turn to the Gentiles.** (The Jews didn't want anything to do with the Word of

God or Jesus. The Word already went to the Jews and they refused to accept Jesus. Now Jesus is sending for the Gentiles or 'Whosoever', in other words, Everyone else.)

47) **For so hath the Lord commanded us,** *saying,* **I have set thee to be a light of the Gentiles, that thou shouldest be for salvation unto the ends of the earth.**   (Jesus as already told the apostles to be a light of the Gentiles.)

48) And when the Gentiles heard this, they were glad, and glorified the word of the Lord: and as many as were ordained to eternal life believed. (Several Gentiles were saved, making them the Bride of Christ and a Jew in the 'Spiritual World' with the Blood of Christ in their veins with all the promises God had made to the Jews who came to Him.)

49) And the word of the Lord was published throughout all the region.

50) But the Jews stirred up the devout and honorable women, and the chief men of the city, and raised persecution against Paul and Barnabas, and expelled them out of their coasts.

51) But they (Paul and Barnabas) shook off the dust of their feet against them, and came unto Iconium.

52) And the disciples were filled with joy, and with the Holy Ghost."

CHURCH BELIEFS

I asked, "What about all the different denominations and church beliefs? Which one is right?" Lay Lay said, "A lot of churches have different beliefs, but there is no one belief that is more important than another. As long as the belief is truly scriptural and founded on the King James Version of the Word of God and they teach the only way for Salvation is to accept Jesus as their Lord and Savior through the Death, Blood and Resurrection of Christ and to serve Jesus with all their heart, strength, and might. Churches are so worried about beliefs and judging they are actually causing division at home, in their own country and it spreads throughout the World. If they can't rule their own cities, states, and countries good how are they supposed to 'go out into all the World and spread the gospel of Jesus?' If their belief is founded on the King James Version of the Word of God, it will edify the Body of Christ. A lot of churches don't really edify the body of Christ, they are edifying the founders of the churches and their own doctrine. A lot of Christians go from one church to another one, especially when they are first starting out in Christianity. They actually spiritually outgrow one church and have to find another one to continue their Spiritual growth in Jesus. A lot of that just depends on where, in Christ, the vessel started to begin with. Don't listen to 'false doctrines' or 'false prophets' though. God gave His Word to humans in the Old and New Testaments, through the Prophets in the Old Testament and through Jesus and the Apostles in the New Testament. There are no more, nor will there be anymore Prophets or Apostles who have written or will write any more testaments for the Most High God. The Alpha and the Omega, the Beginning and the End. God said it all in the Old and New Testaments. The Old and New Testaments are to be used together, not separately."

MOSES
CONTINUED

**(CONTINUED FROM:
HEAVENLY ANGEL LAY LAY
EXPLAINS
WHY CHILDREN AND SPORTS ARE
DEFINITELY A RELIGION IN
TODAY'S
SOCIETY)**

MOSES CONTINUED

Exodus 14:1-31

1) And the LORD spake unto Moses, saying,

2) Speak unto the children of Israel, that they (the children of Israel) turn and encamp before Pihahiroth, between Migdol and the sea, over against Baalzephon: before it (Pihahiroth) shall ye (you) encamp by the sea.

3) For Pharaoh will say of the children of Israel, They (the children of Israel) are entangled in the land, the wilderness hath (has) shut them (the children of Israel) in.

4) And I will harden Pharaoh's heart, that he (Pharaoh) shall (will) follow after them (the children of Israel); and I will be honoured upon Pharaoh, and upon all his host (people); that the Egyptians may know that I am the LORD. And they (Moses and Aaron) did so.

5) And it was told the king of Egypt that the people (the Israelites) fled: and the heart of Pharaoh and of his servants was turned against the people (the Israelites), and they (the Egyptians) said, Why have we done this, that we have let Israel go from serving us (the Egyptians)?

6) And he (Pharaoh) made ready his (Pharaoh's) chariot, and took his (Pharaoh's) people with him (Pharaoh):

7) And **he (Pharaoh) took six hundred (600) chosen**

(especially picked out for this event) chariots, and all the chariots of Egypt, and captains (drivers) over every one of them (the chariots).

8) And the LORD hardened the heart of Pharaoh king of Egypt, and he (Pharaoh) pursued after the children of Israel: and the children of Israel went out with an high hand.

9) But the Egyptians pursued after them (the Israelites), all the horses and chariots of Pharaoh, and his (Pharaoh's) horsemen, and his (Pharaoh's) army, and overtook them (the Israelites) encamping by the sea, beside Pihahiroth, before Baalzephon.

10) And when Pharaoh drew nigh (came close to), the children of Israel lifted up their eyes, and, behold, the Egyptians marched after them (the Israelites); and they (the Israelites) were sore afraid: and the children of Israel cried out unto the LORD.

11) And they (the Israelites) said unto Moses, Because there were no graves in Egypt (the Israelites were alive in Egypt, now the Israelites will die in the wilderness), hast thou taken us away to die in the wilderness? wherefore hast thou (why have you) dealt thus with us (the Israelites), to carry us (the Israelites) forth out of Egypt?

12) Is not this the word that we did tell thee (you) in Egypt, saying, Let us alone (leave the Israelites alone), that we (the Israelites) may serve the Egyptians? For it (our life) had been better for us (the Israelites) to serve the Egyptians, than that we should die in the wilderness. (This is the exact same thing Detta was going through in my book MATTHEW'S WORD 'TWO':REAL WORD OF GOD BIBLE, it's called 'culture shock'. Too much change in a person's life all at once, too far out of a person's 'comfort zone'. The person can't adjust to the sudden change in life.

13) And Moses said unto the people (the Israelites), Fear ye not, stand still, and see the salvation of the LORD, which

he (God) will shew to you (the Israelites) to day: for the Egyptians whom ye (you) have seen to day, ye (you) shall see them (the Egyptians) again no more for ever. (the Israelites will never again see the Egyptians)

14) The LORD shall fight for you (the Israelites), and ye (the Israelites) shall hold your peace.

15) And **the LORD said unto Moses, Wherefore criest thou unto me?** (why do you cry to me?) **speak unto the children of Israel, that they** (tell the children of Israel) **go forward**: (act in faith, you don't have to see the miracle until it's time for the miracle to be needed, not when we want to see the miracle)

16) **But lift thou up thy** (lift up your) **rod, and stretch out thine hand over the sea, and divide it** (divide the sea. God is telling Moses what to do in order to receive the next miracle): **and the children of Israel shall go on dry ground through the midst of the sea**. (now God is telling Moses what the effects of the next miracle will allow the children of Israel do. God is also working directly through Moses now, instead of through Moses and Aaron both)

17) And I, behold, I will harden the hearts of the Egyptians, and they shall follow them (the Israelites): and I will get me honour upon Pharaoh, and upon all his host (Pharaoh's people), upon his (Pharaoh's) chariots, and upon his (Pharaoh's) horsemen.

18) And the Egyptians shall know that I am the LORD, when I have gotten me honour upon Pharaoh, upon his (Pharaoh's) chariots, and upon his (Pharaoh's) horsemen.

19) And the angel of God, which went before the camp of Israel, removed and went behind them (the Israelites); and the pillar of the cloud went from before their (the Israelites) face, and stood behind them (the Israelites):

20) And it (the angel of God and the pillar of the cloud) came between the camp of the Egyptians and the camp of Israel; and it (the pillar) was a cloud and darkness to them

(the Egyptians), but it gave light by night to these (the Israelites): so that the one came not near the other all the night. (the Egyptians could not come near the Israelites all night)

21) And **Moses stretched out his hand over the sea**; and the LORD caused the sea to go back by a strong east wind all that night, and made the sea dry land, and the waters were divided. (here is that east wind again. No wonder the fish don't bite in an east wind)

22) And **the children of Israel went into the midst of the sea upon the dry ground: and the waters were a wall unto them (the Israelites) on their right hand, and on their left. (two walls of water, one on the right and one on the left)** (the effects of the miracle God performed for the children of Israel)

23) And the Egyptians pursued, and went in after them (the Israelites) to the midst of the sea, even all Pharaoh's horses, his chariots, and his horsemen.

24) And it came to pass (eventually), that in the morning watch the LORD looked unto the host (people) of the Egyptians through the pillar of fire and of the cloud, and **troubled the host** (people) of the Egyptians, (gave the Egyptians a lot of trouble)

25) And **took off their** (the Egyptian's) **chariot wheels** (this is what Protecting Angel Shadow and Heavenly Angel Lay Lay were talking about when they were talking about pulling the Egyptian's Chariot's Wheels off the chariots, that is found in my book MATTHEW'S WORD 'TWO':REAL WORD OF GOD BIBLE), that they drave (the Egyptians drove) them heavily (the chariots couldn't move): so that the Egyptians said, Let us flee from the face of Israel; for the LORD fighteth for them (the Israelites) against the Egyptians. (the Egyptians knew the Chariot's Wheels were falling off the Chariots for no human reason)

26) And **the LORD said unto Moses, Stretch out thine**

(your) hand over the sea, that the waters may come again upon the Egyptians, upon their (the Egyptian's) chariots, and upon their (the Egyptian's) horsemen. (God is still only dealing with Moses now. Maybe Aaron had his hands full helping the Israelites getting to the other side of the Red Sea)

27) **And Moses stretched forth his hand over the sea, and the sea returned to his (the sea's) strength when the morning appeared; and the Egyptians fled against it (the waters coming down against the Egyptians); and the LORD overthrew the Egyptians in the midst of the sea.** (Moses again does the actions, not Aaron. Moses's self-worth has gone up drastically since God has been working with him and Moses has been reading God's Word and talking to God on a daily basis)

28) **And the waters returned, and covered the chariots, and the horsemen, and all the host (people and armies) of Pharaoh that came into the sea after them (the Israelites); there remained not so much as one of them (not one person escaped with their life, all were killed).**

29) **But the children of Israel walked upon dry land in the midst of the sea; and the waters were a wall unto them (the Israelites) on their right hand, and on their left.** (the effects of the rest of the miracle)

30) Thus the LORD saved Israel that day out of the hand of the Egyptians; and Israel saw the Egyptians dead upon the sea shore.

31) And Israel saw that great work which the LORD did upon the Egyptians: and the people feared the LORD, and believed the LORD, and his (the Lord's) servant Moses.

Exodus 15:1-27

1) Then sang Moses and the children of Israel this song unto the LORD (the Israelites are rejoicing), and spake, saying, I will sing unto the LORD, for he (the Lord) hath

triumphed gloriously: the horse and his (the horse's) rider hath he (the Lord) thrown into the sea.

2) The LORD is my strength and song, and he (the Lord) is become my salvation: he (the Lord) is my God, and I will prepare him (the Lord) an habitation; my father's God, and I will exalt him (the Lord).

3) The LORD is a man of war: **the LORD is his** (God's) **name**. (here is another example of the Father in Heaven not needing a name, only the creation needs a name, not the creator. The only reason Jesus Christ of Nazareth has a name is because He came down in human form for the remission of our sins, just like Heavenly Angel Lay Lay said, read more about this conversation in my book, MATTHEW'S WORD 'TWO':REAL WORD OF GOD BIBLE. **No where** in this scripture does the name of Jesus appear. The Father's name is **not** Jesus)

4) Pharaoh's chariots and his host (Pharaoh's people) hath he (the Lord) cast into the sea: his (Pharaoh's) chosen captains (the best of all the captains) also are drowned in the Red sea.

5) The depths (water) have (has) covered them (all the Egyptians): they (all Pharaoh's armies) sank into the bottom as a stone (as fast as a stone would sink to the bottom of the sea).

6) Thy (your) right hand, O LORD, is become glorious in power: thy (your) right hand, O LORD, hath dashed in pieces the enemy.

7) And in the greatness of thine (your) excellency thou hast (you have) overthrown them (the Egyptians) that rose up against thee (you): **thou sentest forth (sent) thy (your) wrath (anger),** which consumed them (the Egyptians) as stubble. (Notice God uses the powers of nature to send His anger to destroy the Egyptians). Yes, we see this even today in the weather. God controls the weather, He created the weather, He can use the weather to destroy those who

are against Him.   Of course man can explain how the weather forms, but man can not control when and where the weather strikes)

8) And **with the blast of thy (your) nostrils** (science has it backwards, science needs to <u>disprove</u> that which they don't believe in so they can prove themselves wrong.   Let's see science disprove separating the Red Sea with a blow from His mighty nostrils) **the waters were gathered together, the floods stood upright as an heap, and the depths were congealed (made a wall of water) in the heart of the sea.**

9) The enemy said, I will pursue, I will overtake, I will divide the spoil; my lust shall be satisfied upon them; I will draw my sword, my hand shall destroy them.

10) Thou (you) didst blow with thy (your) wind, the sea covered them (the Egyptians): they (the Egyptians) sank as lead in the mighty waters.

11) Who is like unto thee (you), O LORD, among the gods? who is like thee (you), glorious in holiness, fearful in praises, doing wonders?

12) Thou (you) stretchedst out thy (your) right hand, the earth swallowed them (the Egyptians).

13) Thou (you) in thy (your) mercy hast led forth the people which thou hast redeemed: thou hast (you have) guided them (the Israelites) in thy (your) strength unto thy (your) holy habitation. (God still does guide us in His strength)

14) The people shall hear, and be afraid: sorrow shall take hold on the inhabitants of Palestina (Palestine).

15) Then the dukes (high Princes)of Edom shall be amazed; the mighty men of Moab, trembling shall take hold upon them (the dukes of Edom and the men of Moab); all the inhabitants of Canaan shall melt away.

16) Fear and dread shall fall upon them (all the inhabitants of all the lands); by the greatness of thine (your) arm they (all the inhabitants) shall be as still as a stone; till thy (your) people pass over, O LORD, till the people pass over,

which thou hast (you have) purchased.

17) Thou shalt bring them in, and plant them in the mountain of thine inheritance, in the place, O LORD, which thou hast made for thee to dwell in, in the Sanctuary, O LORD, which thy hands have established.

18) The LORD shall reign for ever and ever.

19) For the horse of Pharaoh went in with his chariots and with his horsemen into the sea, and the LORD brought again the waters of the sea upon them; but the children of Israel went on dry land in the midst of the sea.

20) And <u>Miriam the prophetess, the sister of Aaron</u>, took a timbrel in her hand; and all the women went out after her with timbrels and with dances.

21) And Miriam answered them, Sing ye to the LORD, for he hath triumphed gloriously; the horse and his rider hath he thrown into the sea.

22) So Moses brought Israel from the Red sea, and they (the Israelites) went out into the wilderness of Shur; and they (the Israelites) went three days in the wilderness, and found no water.

23) And when they (the Israelites) came to Marah, they (the Israelites) could not drink of the waters of Marah, for they (the waters) were bitter: therefore the name of it (the waters) was called Marah.

24) And the people murmured against Moses, saying, What shall we drink?

25) And he (Moses) cried unto the LORD; and the LORD shewed him (Moses) a tree, which when he (Moses) had cast into the waters, the waters were made sweet: there he (God) made for them (the Israelites) a statute (law) and an ordinance (law), and there he (God) proved them (the Israelites),

26) And said, If thou wilt diligently hearken (listen) to the voice of the LORD thy God, and wilt do that which is right in his (God's) sight, and wilt give ear to his (God's) commandments, and keep all his (God's) statutes, **I will**

put none of these <u>diseases</u> upon thee (you), which I have brought upon the Egyptians: for I am the LORD that healeth thee.
27) And they (the Israelites) came to Elim, where were twelve wells of water, and threescore and ten palm trees (70 palm trees): and they (the Israelites) encamped there by the waters.

Exodus 16:1-36
1) And they (the Israelites) took their journey from Elim, and all the congregation of the children of Israel came unto the wilderness of Sin, which is between Elim and Sinai, on the **fifteenth day of the second month after their departing out of the land of Egypt**. (75 days, they are making good time considering they have all the possessions of Egypt with them)
2) And the whole congregation of the children of Israel murmured against Moses and Aaron in the wilderness:
3) And the children of Israel said unto them (Moses and Aaron), Would to God we had died by the hand of the LORD in the land of Egypt, when we sat by the flesh pots, and when we did eat bread to the full (to their hearts content); for ye (you) have brought us (the Israelites) forth into this wilderness, to kill this whole assembly with hunger.
4) Then said the LORD unto Moses, Behold, I will rain bread from heaven for you; and the people shall go out and gather a certain rate every day, that I may prove them (the Israelites), whether they (the Israelites) will walk in my (God's) law, or no.
5) And it shall come to pass, that on the sixth day they (the Israelites) shall prepare that which they (the Israelites) bring in; and it (the amount the Israelites bring in) shall be twice as much as they gather daily. (on the seventy day, God will not make it rain bread from Heaven. Gather twice as much as you need for one day on the sixth day because

that amount will need to last you two days instead of one day)

6) And Moses and Aaron said unto all the children of Israel, At even, then ye (you) shall know that the LORD hath brought you out from the land of Egypt:

7) And in the morning, then ye (you) shall see the glory of the LORD; for that he (God) heareth your murmurings (grumblings) against the LORD: and **what are we**, that ye (you) murmur against **us**? (here is a perfect scripture proving there are three parts of the God Head. The terms, **'WE'**, and **'US'**, that's **plural form**. The Father's name is not Jesus Christ of Nazareth, just like Heavenly Angel Lay Lay said in my book MATTHEW'S WORD 'TWO':REAL WORD OF GOD BIBLE)

8) And Moses said, This shall be, when the LORD shall give you in the evening flesh to eat, and in the morning bread to the full; for that the LORD heareth your murmurings (grumbling) which ye (you) murmur against him (God):   and what are we?   your murmurings (grumbling) are not against us, but against the LORD.

9) And **Moses spake unto Aaron**, Say unto all the congregation of the children of Israel, Come near before the LORD: for he (God) hath heard your murmurings. (Aaron is brought into the picture again)

10) And it came to pass, as Aaron spake unto the whole congregation of the children of Israel, that they (the children of Israel) looked toward the wilderness, and, behold, the glory of the LORD appeared in the cloud.

11) And the LORD spake unto Moses, saying,

12) I have heard the murmurings (grumbling) of the children of Israel: speak unto them (the children of Israel), saying, At even ye (you) shall eat flesh, and in the morning ye (you) shall be filled with bread; and ye (you) shall know that I am the LORD your God.

13) And it came to pass, that at even the quails came up, and covered the camp: and in the morning the dew lay

round about the host.

14) And when the dew that lay was gone up, behold, upon the face of the wilderness there lay a small round thing, as small as the hoar frost on the ground.

15) And when the children of Israel saw it, they said one to another, It is manna: for they (the children of Israel) wist not (did not know) what it was. And Moses said unto them, This is the bread which the LORD hath given you to eat.

16) This is the thing which the LORD hath commanded, Gather of it (the bread) every man according to his eating, an omer (an omer is $1/10^{th}$ of an Ephah which is $1/10^{th}$ of a homer which is approximately 220 liters or 6.25 bushels. The homer is a normal load a donkey could carry. So an omer is approximately 2.09 quarts, dry measure) (Holman) for every man, according to the number of your persons; take ye (you) every man for them (your family) which are in his (the man's) tents (notice this word, 'tents', that's plural form, not singular. Each man has a lot of tents because their families are numerous in numbers per household).

17) And the children of Israel did so, and gathered, some more, some less (some families needed more, some families needed less).

18) And when they (the Israelites) did mete it (fill their vessels) with an omer, he that gathered much had nothing over, and he that gathered little had no lack; they gathered every man according to his eating. (a lesson here, as long as we do as God commands to the best of our ability, we will come out just right, no more and no less than what we need)

19) And Moses said, Let no man leave of it (the bread) till the morning.

20) Notwithstanding (never the less) they hearkened not (didn't listen) unto Moses; but some of them (the families) left of it (the bread) until the morning, and it (the bread)

bred worms (had worms in it), and stank: and **Moses was wroth (angry) (my goodness, Moses was only angry twice on the journey to the Promised Land? Once with the Ten Commandments and once at the rock he struck? I don't think so, Moses is angry here too)** with them (those households).

21) And they (the Israelites) gathered it (the bread) every morning, every man according to his eating: and when the sun waxed hot, it (the bread) melted.

22) And it came to pass, that on the sixth day they (the Israelites) gathered twice as much bread, two omers for one man: and all the rulers of the congregation came and told Moses.

23) And he (Moses) said unto them (the rulers of the congregation), This is that which the LORD hath said, To morrow is the rest of the holy sabbath unto the LORD: bake that which ye will bake to day, and seethe (be active) that ye will seethe (be active doing); and that which remaineth over lay up for you to be kept until the morning.

24) And they (the rulers of the congregation) laid it up (the bread) till the morning, as Moses bade (commanded): and it (the bread) did not stink, neither was there any worm therein.

25) And Moses said, Eat that to day; for to day is a sabbath unto the LORD: to day ye (you) shall not find it (any bread) in the field.

26) Six days ye shall gather it (the bread); but on the seventh day, which is the sabbath, in it (the fields) there shall be none (no bread).

27) And it came to pass, that there went out some of the people on the seventh day for to gather, and they (the people who went out to gather the bread) found none (no bread). (always doubters)

28) And the LORD said unto Moses, How long refuse ye to keep my commandments and my laws? (God is testing the Israelites to see if they will obey His commandments and

laws. They didn't, so now He is going to get strict)

29) See, for that the LORD hath given you the sabbath, therefore he (God) giveth you on the sixth day the bread of two days; abide ye every man in his place, let no man go out of his place on the seventh day. (now God is restricting every man to his tent on the seventy day. A punishment for leaving the tents and going to the fields looking for bread on the seventh day)

30) So the people rested on the seventh day. (now God has their attention and the people are obeying Him)

31) And the house of Israel called the name thereof Manna: and it was like coriander seed, white; and the taste of it (the bread from Heaven) was like wafers made with honey.

32) And Moses said, This is the thing which the LORD commandeth, Fill an omer of it (the bread from Heaven) to be kept for your generations; that they (your generations) may see the bread wherewith I have fed you in the wilderness, when I brought you forth from the land of Egypt.

33) And Moses said unto Aaron, Take a pot, and put an omer full of manna therein, and lay it (the omer of manna) up before the LORD, to be kept for your generations.

34) As the LORD commanded Moses, so Aaron laid it (the omer of manna) up before the Testimony, to be kept.

35) And **the children of Israel did eat manna <u>forty years</u>** (talk about a strict diet of bread), until they (the children of Israel) came to a land inhabited (lived in by other people or animals, in this case though the land was lived in by people); they (the children of Israel) did eat manna, until they (the Israelites) came unto the borders of the land of Canaan.

36) Now an omer is the tenth part of an ephah (an ephah is $1/10^{th}$ of a homer which is approximately 220 liters or 6.25 bushels. So an ephah is approximately 22 liters or .625 bushels)

Exodus 17:1-16

1) And all the congregation of the children of Israel journeyed from the wilderness of Sin, after their journeys (you notice 'journeys' is plural form? That means the trip took more than one day), according to the commandment of the LORD, and pitched in Rephidim: and there was no water for the people to drink.

2) Wherefore the people did chide (get angry) with Moses, and said, Give us water that we may drink. And Moses said unto them, Why chide ye (are you angry) with me? wherefore do ye (you) tempt the LORD?

3) And the people thirsted there for water; and the people murmured against Moses, and said, Wherefore is this that thou hast (you have) brought us up out of Egypt, to kill us and our children and our cattle with thirst?

4) And Moses cried unto the LORD, saying, What shall I do unto this people? they be almost ready to stone me.

5) And the LORD said unto Moses, Go on before the people, and take with thee of (you) the elders of Israel; and thy (your) rod, wherewith (the rod that) thou (you) smotest (hit, dipped into) the river, take in thine (your) hand, and go.

6) Behold, I will stand before thee (you) there upon the rock in Horeb; and thou (you) shalt smite (hit) the rock, and there shall come water out of it, that the people may drink. And Moses did so in the sight of the elders of Israel. (now you notice God wanted Moses to do all this while the elders of Israel watched)

7) And he (Moses) called the name of the place Massah, and Meribah, because of the chiding (scolding) of the children of Israel, and because they (the children of Israel) tempted the LORD, saying, Is the LORD among us, or not?

8) Then came Amalek, and fought with Israel in Rephidim.

9) And Moses said unto Joshua, Choose us out men, and go out, fight with Amalek: to morrow I will stand on the top of the hill with the rod of God in mine hand.

10) So Joshua did as Moses had said to him, and fought with Amalek: and Moses, Aaron, and Hur went up to the top of the hill.   (you notice there are two people with Moses. God did this for a reason. God was going to put all three men to work)

11) And it came to pass (eventually), when Moses held up his hand, that Israel prevailed: and when he (Moses) let down his hand, Amalek prevailed. (notice the only time the children of Israel was winning was when Moses was raising his hand toward HEAVEN. That gives us a huge clue about what God wants us to do, doesn't it?)

12) But Moses hands were heavy; and they (Aaron and Hur) took a stone, and put it (the stone) under him (Moses), and he (Moses) sat thereon; and Aaron and Hur stayed up hands (helped Moses keep his hands up), the one on the one side, and the other on the other side; and his (Moses) hands were steady (constantly up toward Heaven) until the going down of the sun. (all day. That is why God told Moses to take Aaron and Hur with him. To help erect the rock and help Moses keep his arms toward Heaven. God wanted them to put effort into the battle for the victory. Reminds me of people after hours and hours of prayer, finally praying through to victory)

13) And Joshua discomfited (killed) Amalek and his people with the edge of the sword.

14) And the LORD said unto Moses, Write this for a memorial in a book, and rehearse it in the ears of Joshua: for I will utterly put out the remembrance of Amalek from under heaven.

15) And Moses built an altar, and called the name of it Jehovahnissi:

16) For he (Moses) said, Because the LORD hath sworn that the LORD will have war with Amalek from generation to generation.

Exodus 18:1-27

1) When Jethro, the priest of Midian, Moses' father in law, heard of all that God had done for Moses, and for Israel his people, and that the LORD had brought Israel out of Egypt;

2) Then Jethro, Moses' father in law, took Zipporah, Moses' wife, after he (Moses) had sent her (Zipporah, Moses wife) back (to Jethro),

3) And her (Zipporah) two sons; of which the name of the one was Gershom; for he (Moses) said, I have been an alien in a strange land:

4) And the name of the other was Eliezer; for the God of my father, said he (Moses said), was mine help, and delivered me (Moses) from the sword of Pharaoh: (if you haven't caught on, Moses named his two sons after two different reason at the time each son was born according to what Moses was going through at the time of each of their birth)

5) And Jethro, Moses' father in law, came with his (Moses) sons and his (Moses) wife unto Moses into the wilderness, where he encamped (Moses was camping) at the mount of God:

6) And he (Jethro) said unto Moses, I thy (your) father in law Jethro am come unto thee (you), and thy (your) wife, and her (Zipporah's) two sons with her (Zipporah). (Jethro is bringing Moses wife, Zipporah and Moses two sons Gershom, and Eliezer back to Moses)

7) And Moses went out to meet his father in law, and did obeisance (honored), and kissed him (Zipporah); and they (Moses and Zipporah) asked each other of their welfare (how each of them were doing); and they (Moses and Zipporah) came into the tent.

8) And Moses told his father in law (Jethro) all that the LORD had done unto Pharaoh and to the Egyptians for Israel's sake, and all the travail (problems) that had come upon them (the children of Israel) by the way, and how the LORD delivered them (the children of Israel).

9) And Jethro rejoiced for all the goodness which the

LORD had done to Israel, whom he (God) had delivered out of the hand of the Egyptians.

10) And Jethro said, Blessed be the LORD, who hath delivered you out of the hand of the Egyptians, and out of the hand of Pharaoh, who hath delivered the people from under the hand of the Egyptians.

11) Now I know (this is interesting, there was doubt in Jethro's mind about who really was the most High God, see the phrase, 'Now I know'. That shows there was doubt in Jethro's mind) that the LORD is greater than all gods: for in the thing wherein they (the Egyptians) dealt proudly he (God) was above them (Egypt and all their gods).

12) And Jethro, Moses' father in law, took a burnt offering and sacrifices for God: and Aaron came, and all the elders of Israel, to eat bread with Moses' father in law before God.

13) And it came to pass on the morrow, that Moses sat to judge the people: and the people stood by Moses from the morning unto the evening.

14) And when Moses' father in law (Jethro) saw all that he (Moses) did to the people, he (Jethro) said, What is this thing that thou (Moses) doest to the people? why sittest thou thyself alone (why is Moses sitting alone?), and all the people stand by (wait for) thee (you) from morning unto even?

15) And Moses said unto his father in law, Because the people come unto me to enquire of God:

16) When they (someone from the tribe) have a matter, they (the two or more who have a matter that needs resolved) come unto me (Moses); and I judge between one and another, and I do make them (the ones with the problem) know the statutes (commandments) of God, and his (God's) laws.

17) And Moses' father in law said unto him (Moses), The thing that thou (Moses) doest (does) is not good.

18) Thou (Moses) wilt surely wear away (Moses will wear himself out), both thou (Moses), and this people that is with

thee (all that are with Moses): for this thing (burden) is too heavy for thee (Moses); thou art (you are) not able to perform it (all the problem solving) thyself alone.

19) Hearken (listen) now unto my (Jethro's) voice, I will give thee (Moses) counsel, and God shall be with thee (Moses): Be thou for the people to God-ward (lead the people to God, give the people Godly wisdom), that thou mayest (Moses may) bring the causes (problems) unto God:

20) And thou (Moses) shalt teach them (the children of Israel) ordinances and laws, and shalt shew them (show the children of Israel) the way wherein they (the children of Israel) must walk, and the work that they (the children of Israel) must do.

21) Moreover thou (Moses) shalt provide out of all the people able **men** (notice **this is specific, Christian, God fearing, men who know the King James Version of the Word of God, not women**), such as fear (see? God Fearing) God, **men of truth** (a man of truth must know the King James Version of the Word of God. That's the only Real Word of God Bible on the market today according to Heavenly Angel Lay Lay. If you don't know who Heavenly Angel Lay Lay is, then you need to purchase my book, "MATTHEW'S WORD 'TWO':REAL WORD OF GOD BIBLE", hating covetousness; and place such (those **Christian, God fearing, men who know the King James Version of the Word of God**) over them (the children of Israel), to be rulers (in charge) of thousands (only **Christian, God fearing, men who know the King James Version of the Word of God** as judges in Federal Courts), and rulers (in charge) of hundreds (only **Christian, God fearing, men who know the King James Version of the Word of God** as judges in State Courts), rulers (in charge) of fifties (only **Christian, God fearing, men who know the King James Version of the Word of God** as judges in County Courts), and rulers (in charge) of tens (only

Christian, God fearing, men who know the King James Version of the Word of God as judges in City Courts):

22) And let them (the **Christian, God fearing, men who know the King James Version of the Word of God** in charge) judge the people at all seasons (year around): and it shall be, that every great matter (big problem) they (the **Christian, God fearing, men who know the King James Version of the Word of God** in charge of the smaller amount of people) shall bring unto thee (Moses), but every small matter they (the **Christian, God fearing, men who know the King James Version of the Word of God** in charge of the smaller amount of people) shall judge: so shall it (the judging) be easier for thyself (Moses), and they (the **Christian, God fearing, men who know the King James Version of the Word of God** in charge of the smaller amounts of people) shall bear the burden with thee (Moses).

23) If thou (Moses) shalt do this thing, and God command thee (you) so, then thou (Moses) shalt be able to endure, and all this people shall also go to their place in peace.

24) So Moses hearkened (listened) to the voice of his father in law (Jethro), and did all that he (Jethro) had said.

25) And **Moses chose able men** (not one woman was in charge or ruled anyone) out of all Israel, and made them (the **Christian, God fearing, men who know the King James Version of the Word of God**) heads over the people, rulers of thousands (only **Christian, God fearing, men who know the King James Version of the Word of God** as judges in Federal Courts), rulers of hundreds (only **Christian, God fearing, men who know the King James Version of the Word of God** as judges in State Courts), rulers of fifties (only **Christian, God fearing, men who know the King James Version of the Word of God** as judges in County Courts), and rulers of tens (only **Christian, God fearing, men who know the King James**

Version of the Word of God as judges in City Courts).
26) And they (the **Christian, God fearing, men who know the King James Version of the Word of God**) judged the people at all seasons: the hard causes they (the **Christian, God fearing, men who know the King James Version of the Word of God** in charge) brought unto Moses, but every small matter they (the **Christian, God fearing, men who know the King James Version of the Word of God** in charge) judged themselves. (a lot of people may wonder why people in churches don't go to the elders of the churches when their members have a disagreement like the Bible commands us to. A lot of members of other social clubs go to their elders when they have a disagreement even in cases of adultery, other social clubs cover the disagreement up instead of going to the authorities or the attorneys. Here is a good example of the reason members of churches don't go to the elders of that church when there are disputes among the members. One church I went to years ago, there were a group of close teenagers, which is good, one of the parents of a teenager in that group drove them around. Most of the teens had to climb in the back of the pickup with a canopy on it. This went on for several months, no one complained, all the mothers knew it was going on, but everyone was content with the mother driving everyone around even in the back of the pickup with the canopy. The teens always had a good time. Then one day for some reason the canopy flew off and hurt a couple of the teens. Sure there was insurance, that wasn't the problem. The teens who were injured were checked out and releases within a few hours. The incident scared everyone more than it hurt anyone. Situation solved, right? Wrong, it seems like the mother of one of the teens who were frightened and hurt a little went in front of the elders of the church to see what the church suggested, God forbid her child be frightened and a scratch on that teen in care of

another mother. It wasn't even a church event. Well, the elders of the church got together and there were some wise men on that church board. They saw all the evidence and heard from everyone involved. The only teens and mother who really wanted to pursue this was that particular mother had her teens. None of the other teens involved or their mothers thought much about it, it was an unfortunate accident, but everyone knew it was going on and the teens enjoyed being together to have fellowship. The fathers and mothers loved seeing the unity of the teens like that and most importantly, the fathers and mothers knew their children were ok and having fun. They didn't worry about their children getting drunk, having sex, or on drugs. The parents were relieved that the teens enjoyed being together with a good chaperone, someone the fathers and mothers trusted from the church every few nights. The elders of the church came back and announced there was nothing more than needed to be done since the teens who were injured were already taken care of from the medical standpoint and within a few hours were released from the doctor's care. The medication the doctor did prescribe was taken care of by the mother's insurance so everything was taken care of. The fathers and mothers would need to stop using a pickup and canopy to transport the teens around though. The mother wasn't satisfied with that because she had already seen an attorney and the attorney was already talking to her about damages from the pain and suffering her child went through. The mother finally went and filed civil charges against the mother who was driving that day and it was settled out of court. The problem is why is a Christian listening to Satan? All that attorney is out for is their percentage or their fee. They don't care about our children. She went to see what the elders of the church advised and when their advise didn't suit her, she went to Satan to get money. That's why a lot of the members of church don't go to the elders of the church any longer. When the elders of the church do give good Biblical Advice, the members don't accept the advice anyway. That mother totally ruined a good thing for everyone because she was more interested in money than her teen being around other teen Christians and the peace of mind knowing her teen was being taken care of and watched out for by other members of her church. Of course there were hard feelings among the teens after that. The first thing the attorney is going to advice is don't talk about the case to anyone and what teen is going to be able to do that around their friends when the subject comes up? So by the advice of the attorney, her teens had to finally drop out of the teen group at church and eventually stopped going to church all together. Satan sure did use that attorney and mother to destroy something good God had going in that teen group in that church, didn't he. The mother was seeing dollar signs where the elders of the church were seeing the unity of the church and the unity of the teens)

27) And Moses let his father in law (Jethro) depart; and he (Jethro) went his way into his (Jethro's) own land.

Exodus 19:1-25

1) In the third month, when the children of Israel were gone forth out of the land of Egypt, the same day came they into the wilderness of Sinai. (in other words the third month to the day they went from Egypt and arrived in the wilderness of Sinai)

2) For they (the children of Egypt) were departed from Rephidim, and were come to the desert of Sinai, and had pitched in the wilderness; and there Israel camped before the mount.

3) And Moses went up unto God, and the LORD called unto him (Moses) out of the mountain, saying, Thus shalt thou (Moses) say to the house of Jacob (the children of Israel), and tell the children of Israel;

4) Ye have seen (the children of Israel has seen) what I

(God) did unto the Egyptians, and how I (God) bare you (the children of Israel) on eagles' wings, and brought you (the children of Israel) unto myself (God).

5) Now therefore, **if** ye (the children of Israel) will **obey my (God's) voice** indeed, and **keep my (God's) covenant, then** ye **(the Children of Israel) shall be a peculiar (special) treasure unto me (God) above all people**: for all the earth is mine: (this particular scripture is exactly what Heavenly Angel Lay Lay was talking about when she said the children of Israel was God's Chosen People as long as they obeyed His laws and commandments, but , as a nation, they went back to idolatry, worshipping the idols of Egypt and are no longer God's Chosen People. Now God judges them just like anyone else, on an individual basis. See the stipulation here? More about this subject in my book MATTHEW'S WORD 'TWO':REAL WORD OF GOD BIBLE)

6) And ye (the children of Israel) shall be unto me (God) a kingdom of priests, and an holy nation. These are the words which thou shalt (you will) speak unto the children of Israel.

7) And Moses came and called for the elders of the people, and laid before their (the elders) faces all these words which the LORD commanded him (Moses).

8) And all the people answered together, and said, All that the LORD hath spoken we will do. And Moses returned the words of the people unto the LORD.

9) And the LORD said unto Moses, Lo, I come unto thee (Moses) in a thick cloud, that the people (the children of Israel) may hear when I (God) speak with thee (Moses), and believe thee (Moses) for ever. And Moses told the words of the people unto the LORD. (God is going to expose His voice to all the children of Israel so everyone can hear God speak to Moses)

10) And the LORD said unto Moses, Go unto the people, and sanctify (cleanse) them (the children of Israel) to day

and to morrow, and let them (the children of Israel) wash their clothes,

11) And be ready against the third day: for the third day the LORD will come down in the sight of all the people upon mount Sinai.

12) And thou (Moses) shalt set bounds unto the people round about, saying, Take heed to yourselves, that ye go not (you do not go) up into the mount, or touch the border of it (the mount): **whosoever toucheth** the mount **shall be surely put to death**: (you notice it doesn't say the person will die instantly or automatically, but they will be 'put to death')

13) There shall not an hand touch it (the mount), but he (anyone or any animal) shall surely be stoned, or shot through; (the Israelites were to kill the person or beast that touched even the border of the mount) whether it be beast or man, it shall not live: when the trumpet soundeth long, they (the Israelites) shall come up to the mount.

14) And Moses went down from the mount unto the people, and sanctified (cleansed) the people; and they (the Israelites) washed their clothes.

15) And he (Moses) said unto the people, Be ready against the third day: come not at your wives. (they weren't even supposed to make love to their wives beforehand, the cleansing, or sanctification would be gone)

16) And it came to pass on the third day in the morning, that there were thunders and lightnings, and a thick cloud (the Father in Heaven, God) upon the mount, and the voice of the trumpet exceeding loud; so that all the people that was in the camp trembled.

17) And Moses brought forth the people out of the camp to meet with God; and they (the Israelites) stood at the nether part of the mount.

18) And mount Sinai was altogether on a smoke, because the LORD descended (came down) upon it (the mount) in fire: and the smoke thereof ascended (went up) as the

smoke of a furnace, and the whole mount quaked greatly.

19) And when the voice of the trumpet sounded long, and waxed louder and louder, Moses spake, and God answered him (Moses) by a voice. (notice the scripture says, 'by a voice', not the voice of God, but an audible voice Moses could hear and understand)

20) And the LORD came down upon mount Sinai, on the top of the mount: and the LORD called Moses up to the top of the mount; and Moses went up.

21) And the LORD said unto Moses, Go down, charge (command) the people, lest (or else) they break through unto the LORD to gaze (see the Lord), and many of them (whoever or whatever touches the mount) perish (die). (God is protecting the people, He knows His supernatural power would kill the people)

22) And let the priests also, which come near to the LORD, sanctify themselves (even the priests have to sanctify themselves), lest (or else) the LORD break forth (kill) upon them.

23) And Moses said unto the LORD, The people cannot come up to mount Sinai: for thou chargedst (you commanded) us (Moses, Aaron, and Hur), saying, Set bounds about the mount, and sanctify it.

24) And the LORD said unto him (Moses), Away, get thee down, and thou shalt come up, thou, and Aaron with thee (Moses): but let not the priests and the people break through to come up unto the LORD, lest he (God) break forth upon them (anyone else).

25) So Moses went down unto the people, and spake unto them (the people).

Exodus 20:1-26

1) And God spake all these words, saying,

2) I am the LORD thy God, which have brought thee (you) out of the land of Egypt, out of the house of bondage.

3) Thou shalt have no other gods before me. (including

children and sports. Children or sports are not to be in anyone's life before God. God first, spouse second, children third and job/career fourth, just like Heavenly Angel Lay Lay said, more about that in my book MATTHEW'S WORD 'TWO':REAL WORD OF GOD BIBLE)

4) Thou shalt not make unto thee any graven image, or any likeness of any thing that is in heaven above, or that is in the earth beneath, or that is in the water under the earth.

5) Thou shalt not bow down thyself to them, nor serve them (including the statue of Mary, the mother of Jesus. Just like Heavenly Angel Lay Lay explained): for I the LORD thy (your) God am a jealous (see, God is jealous and wrathful, that means God has a temper, God gets angry. People say being jealous is of Satan, jealousy is not good, yes it is in the right perspective, God can't do anything evil, doing evil is against His character. Remember, Satan can only take that which God created and make it evil. God created jealousy, not Satan. Satan doesn't have the power to create anything) God, visiting the iniquity (sins) of the fathers upon the children unto the third and fourth generation of them that hate me;

6) And shewing (showing) mercy unto thousands of them that love me, and keep my commandments.

7) Thou shalt not take the name of the LORD thy God in vain; for the LORD will not hold him guiltless that taketh his name in vain. (we need to remember, God is talking to the Israelites here. That means even a Christian who takes the name of the Lord in vain is in deep, deep trouble. Jesus may have taken our sins away by His Blood, but after we are sanctified the first time, we are held accountable for everything thereafter and that will be done on Judgment Day)

8) Remember the sabbath day, to keep it holy. (now a lot of churches keep the day of Resurrection holy)

9) Six days shalt thou labour, and do all thy work: (this

hasn't changed, so all those plants and people working overtime seven days a week are sinning with the exception of witnessing and ministering. Why those two? Jesus did use the parable about rescuing an animal that strayed from the flock on the seventy day, remember?

10) But the seventh day is the sabbath of the LORD thy God: in it thou shalt not do any work, thou, nor thy son, nor thy daughter, thy manservant, nor thy maidservant, nor thy cattle, nor thy stranger that is within thy gates: (no man, woman, or animal shall do work in the Sabbath, or day of resurrection)

11) For in six days the LORD made heaven and earth, the sea, and all that in them is, and rested the seventh day: wherefore the LORD blessed the sabbath day, and hallowed it (made it holy. Remember, that's why the deception of Eve that caused the fall of mankind couldn't have happened on the seventh day, the serpent was resting and Adam was resting at home instead of working on the seventh day as God had commanded).

12) Honour thy father and thy mother: that thy days may be long upon the land which the LORD thy God giveth thee.

13) Thou shalt not kill. (this one a lot of people get confused about. Not killing is taking someone out and taking their life for no biblical reason. When people commit adultery and are stoned, that's not considered killing, but judgment. In today's words, if a person is convicted and sentenced to death, then it's not killing because the death is due to a sentence for the conviction of a crime not just to kill them)

14) Thou shalt not commit adultery. (This on is explained in full detail in my book, 'MATTHEW'S WORD 'TWO':REAL WORD OF GOD BIBLE)

15) Thou shalt not steal. (stealing is almost as bad as adultery)

16) Thou shalt not bear false (wrong accusations, wrongly

accuse, lie about them) witness against thy neighbour.

17) Thou shalt not covet thy neighbour's house, thou shalt not covet thy neighbour's wife, nor his manservant, nor his maidservant, nor his ox, nor his ass, nor any thing that is thy neighbour's. (notice this is right below 'bearing false witness against your neighbor'?   If you want your neighbors wife or house or anything they own, one may think of ways to get rid of your neighbor that is just short of killing them. If you don't want someone elses stuff, then you will have no reason to lie about them)

18) And all the people (the Israelites) saw the thunderings, and the lightnings, and the noise of the trumpet, and the mountain smoking: and when the people saw it, they removed (they high-tailed it out of that area, they were afraid), and stood afar off (a long ways away).

19) And they (the Israelites) said unto Moses, Speak thou with us (now the Israelites want Moses to speak to them instead of God), and we will hear: but let not God speak with us, lest we die. (the Israelites are afraid of dieing because of the Supernatural Power of God's voice)

20) And Moses said unto the people (the Israelites), Fear not: for God is come to prove you, and that his (God's) fear may be before your faces (the faces of the Israelites), that ye sin not. (now why would God be fearful? God doesn't want the Israelites to burn in Hell, He fears they will unless they do as He commands and follow Him as their God)

21) And the people stood afar off, and Moses drew near unto the **thick darkness** where God was. (here is an interesting passage. God is in 'the thick darkness'. God isn't always in light)

22) And the LORD said unto Moses, Thus thou shalt say unto (Moses shall say to) the children of Israel, Ye (you) have seen that I have talked with you from heaven.

23) Ye (you) shall not make with me gods of silver (God doesn't want us to create His image out of silver), neither

shall ye (you) make unto you gods of gold. [no graven images of any god. This must be really important, God said it twice now. (It is really important, demons can live in statues and images of gods from Satan. Any god that is not the Father in Heaven, Jesus Christ of Nazareth and the Holy Spirit from Heaven is a god from Satan. Read more about this in my book MATTHEW'S WORD 'TWO':REAL WORD OF GOD BIBLE)]

24) <u>An altar **of earth**</u> (God is being specific about what He wants, an alter of Earth. God uses a Wicca God, a God of Nature, or what others call, 'Mother Earth', for His alter. God is using a 'false god' for His alter) God is telling Moses to build the alter for God out of EARTH. This should tell a lot of people how strong the Supernatural Power of God really is) thou (you) shalt make unto me, and shalt sacrifice thereon (God is telling Moses to take the sacrifice and actually make the sacrifice on the 'false god', God is using the 'false god' as a slab for His sacrifice) thy burnt offerings, and thy peace offerings, thy sheep, and thine oxen: **in all places** (this covers the whole Earth, the planets, all the universes, Heaven, Hell, the Great Gulf, all places covers the known and unknown places as well) where I record my name (where God is known, that covers infinity, everywhere, He created everything, He is known throughout everywhere. Wherever we can and can not see, hear, touch, feel, even imagine) I will come unto thee (no matter where we are, He will come to us, even throughout infinity), and I will bless thee. (He will bless us, that's His promise to all the Israelites and all Christians are Israelites in the Spiritual World, that's a part of the 'Spiritual Bloodline', read more about this in my book, MATTHEW'S WORD 'TWO':REAL WORD OF GOD BIBLE, and God must keep His promise to us)

25) And if thou wilt make me an altar of stone, thou shalt not build it of hewn (cut or carved, anything other than the raw material) stone: for if thou (you) lift up thy tool upon

it (if you try to create something with the stone), thou hast polluted it (you have destroyed it's worth to me) (God wants the raw material so He can create something that He wants from that raw material without our carnal minds interfering).

26) Neither shalt thou (you) go up by steps unto mine altar (God is telling Moses to stay off the alter), that thy (Moses) nakedness (without going through something else) be not discovered thereon. (in other words, Moses can not see God without God going through someone or something that Moses carnal mind can handle, if Moses saw God's real self, God's nakedness, Moses carnal mind would go crazy and die, Moses couldn't handle the Supernatural Power of God just like I couldn't handle all the Supernatural Power of Jesus Christ of Nazareth when I was allowed to see His 'fiery red eyes' and 'the hem of His Throne Room Robe', the Holy Spirit had to control how much of His Supernatural Powers I was allowed to see before the Holy Spirit turned those Supernatural Colors to black and white. That's in my book, 'MATTHEW'S WORD 'TWO':REAL WORD OF GOD BIBLE

(CONTINUED IN: HEAVENLY ANGEL LAY LAY AND PROTECTING ANGEL SHADOW GUESS THE REAL AGE OF THE EARTH)

BIBLIOGRAPHY

1. Encarta ® World English Dictionary © & (P) 1998-2004 Microsoft Corporation. All rights reserved.

2. Merriam Webster's Collegiate Dictionary Tenth Edition (1993), United States of America.

3. The Holy Bible King James Version (1998), B. B. Kirkbride Bible Co., Inc. Indianapolis, IN..USA

4. Holman Bible Dictionary (1991), Holman Bible Publishers, Nashville, Tennessee.